Cryptocurrency Primer

Everything You Need to Know About

Cryptocurrencies and How They Are Different from

Regular (Fiat) Money (With Mining Guides for

Bitcoin, Ethereum, Litecoin and ZCash)

I0481496

Cryptocurrency Primer

Copyright ©2018 by (Tom J. Bernstein)

ISBN-13: 978-1985089693

ISBN-10: 1985089696

Table of Contents

Chapter 3- Cryptocurrencies vs. Fiat Money101

Conclusion.. 107

Introduction

The need for cryptocurrencies is on the rise. Most businesses are now adding various cryptocurrencies as a means of payment. Cryptocurrencies have been developing, and there are now around 700 available throughout the world. A number of benefits are associated with the use of cryptocurrencies compared to fiat money. When making payments with cryptocurrencies, a small fee is charged. In some cases, the amount charged is almost insignificant. Cryptocurrency transactions can also be completed within a short period of time, nearly in real time. This is why banks are beginning to rely on them to make cross-border payments. It is also possible to complete cryptocurrency transactions faster due to the ease of the verification process compared to using fiat money. Cryptocurrencies are capable of regulating themselves, and they do not suffer from inflation. A major feature of cryptocurrencies, which has attracted a great attention from all the world, is the fact that they do not rely on any central authority for management or regulation. This is a feature most institutions such as banks have wanted but have not been able to implement. Most organizations in various industries are looking for a way to tap into and benefit from it. This book explores the various aspects of cryptocurrencies. Enjoy reading!

Chapter 1- What is Cryptocurrency?

Cryptocurrency refers to a virtual or digital currency that relies on cryptography for security. Due to such a security feature, it is hard to counterfeit cryptocurrency. Cryptocurrencies are not issued by any central bank, making them free from interference by any government. This means that cryptocurrencies do not rely on the control of a centralized authority such as a government, bank or other institution. They are capable of regulating themselves.

Cryptocurrency transactions are anonymous in nature, making cryptocurrencies a suitable option for activities such as tax evasion and money laundering. Bitcoin is known to be the first cryptocurrency launched in 2009 by an individual using the pseudonym *Satoshi Nakamoto*. In 2015, there were about 14.6 million bitcoins in circulation. This is equal to a market value of about $13.4 billion. The success of Bitcoin in the market has seen the rise of other cryptocurrencies such as Litecoin, PPCoin, NameCoin, etc.

Cryptocurrencies have made it easy for us to transfer funds between parties. The transfer of funds is facilitated by use of private and public keys. The transfers normally incur fewer transaction fees, helping cryptocurrency users avoid the heavy fees charged for transfers in banks and other financial institutions for wire transfers.

Blockchain technology is the technology underlying Bitcoin. It provides a public ledger in which all Bitcoin transactions can be recorded. The technology provides the ledger with a data structure that is copyable on all computers running Bitcoin software. The ledger is also less exposed to the threat of hacker attack. Such a technology has been found to be very useful in areas such as crowdfunding, electronic voting, etc. The technology is also very important for financial institutions as it can help them lower transaction fees and come up with a more efficient way of carrying on transactions. Note that the prices of cryptocurrencies are not determined by any centralized authority, but by the forces of demand and supply. This is why the prices of cryptocurrencies fluctuate widely. A good example is Bitcoin.

Although it is hard for one to hack into cryptocurrencies, they are not immune to it. Several people and companies have been reported to have lost money through online theft by hackers. Despite this, the majority of observers have seen that cryptocurrencies offer hope that currencies can exist that preserve value, facilitate exchange and become more transportable compared to hard metal; and at the same time it is not influenced by governments or the central bank.

Cryptocurrencies are simply limited entries in a database that one is not able to change without meeting a number of conditions. Consider the money you have stored in your bank account. What is it in reality? It is simply entries made into a database that can only be changed under specific conditions.

A cryptocurrency such as Bitcoin is made up of a network of nodes. Every node on the network has access to the history of all the transactions that have happened, hence they can know the balances of each account.

A transaction is simply a file saying, "Alice gives X bitcoins to Bob," that is signed using the private key of Alice. It is just basic public key cryptography. Once it has been signed, the transaction is broadcasted on the network, then sent from one peer to the other peer. That is how the basic p2p technology works.

The entire network knows about the transaction almost immediately. However, it is only confirmed after a particular time. Confirmation is a very important process in cryptocurrencies as they can be said to be all about confirmation. It is the process through which the nodes can tell whether a transaction is legitimate or not.

If the transaction has not been confirmed, it is in a pending state and can be forged. Once a transaction has been confirmed, it cannot be reversed; it cannot be forged as it becomes part of immutable record of historical transactions.

The work of *miners* in the cryptocurrency network is to confirm transactions. This is done by taking transactions, stamping them as legit then spreading them to the cryptocurrency network. Once a miner has confirmed a transaction, the other nodes in the network should add it to the database. It then becomes part of the blockchain.

The miners normally work for the job they do, and the reward is in the form of a token of cryptocurrency such as bitcoins.

Anyone is allowed to be a miner in the blockchain. Note that in the cryptocurrency network, there is no centralized authority who can delegate the tasks; thus, the network should have a mechanism of preventing any single person from abusing the system. Somebody may create thousands of peers, then use them to spread forged transactions. This can break the system immediately.

Satoshi set the cryptocurrency network in such a way that miners must invest some work on their computers to qualify for the task. They are expected to find the hash, which results from a cryptographic function connecting the new block to the predecessor. The process is known as *proof-of-work*. In Bitcoin, this depends on SHA 256 Hash algorithm.

As a miner, you are not expected to know details regarding the SHA 256 Hash algorithm. You only have to know that miners are involved in solving some cryptographic puzzles after which they earn a reward. Once a miner has found a solution, he can create a block then add it to the blockchain. Note that these miners compete to do this and the first one to solve the puzzle is rewarded in the form of a token of cryptocurrency.

The process of mining brings bitcoins back into circulation. Without solving the cryptographic puzzles, we cannot have bitcoins in circulation. To control inflation, the process of mining bitcoins becomes harder as more miners join the Bitcoin network. This is why Bitcoin is self-regulating. The currency is not expected to suffer inflation. There is also regulation of the amount of bitcoins that can be created over a particular period of time.

Basically, cryptocurrencies are simply entries about a token in a decentralized consensus database. They are referred to as cryptocurrencies since the process of reaching a consensus is secure via strong cryptography. These cryptocurrencies are built on cryptography. They are secured by math rather than by trust or people.

Transactional Properties of Cryptocurrencies

Most cryptocurrencies share same properties, as described below:

1. Irreversibility

    Once a transaction has been confirmed, it can't be reversed. Nobody, despite their authority, can reverse a cryptocurrency transaction that has been confirmed. After sending cryptocurrency such as bitcoins, there is no way for you to get them back. If you send your money to a scammer or a hacker steals your cryptocurrency, there is no way for you to recover it.

2. Pseudonymous

   Neither the accounts nor the transactions are connected to real-world identities. Bitcoins are received at addresses, which are just strings of about 30 characters. It is possible for one to analyze the flow of the transactions, but it is impossible to link them to any real-world identity of users.

3. Security

   Cryptocurrency transactions are secured via means of public key cryptography. Only the person who owns the private key for the wallet can send money/cryptocurrency. The system relies on strong cryptography algorithms and the magic of using big numbers so that it may make it hard to break it. A Bitcoin address is more secure as compared to Fork Knox. The only way for one to steal your cryptocurrency is to know your private key, which you can secure for the sake of your cryptocurrency.

4. Fast and Global

The propagation of the transactions in the network is done almost instantly and the confirmation is done within minutes. This is done within a network of computers located in all parts of the globe, meaning that the location of your computer does not matter. You can send bitcoins to your neighbor or even to someone located on the other side of the world.

5. Permissionless

   You are not required to ask anyone to make use
   of cryptocurrency. It is software that anyone
   can download without paying for it. After
   installing it on your computer, you will be able
   to receive and send bitcoins as well as other
   cryptocurrencies. There is no gatekeeper,
   meaning that no one can prevent it.

Monetary Properties of Cryptocurrencies

1. Controlled supply

   The majority of cryptocurrencies normally limit
   the supply of tokens. In the case of Bitcoin, the
   supply normally reduces with time, and it is
   expected to reach the final numbers about
   2140. In all cryptocurrencies, the supply of
   tokens is controlled via a schedule
   implemented in the code. This means that it is

possible for us to calculate now the supply of any cryptocurrency tokens at any particular future moment.

2. No debt but bearer

   The fiat money in your bank account has been created by debt, and the numbers seen on the account balance are simply debts. This is different with cryptocurrencies as they don't represent debt, but they represent themselves. They are hard money just like gold coins.

For you to know more about the revolutionary impact of cryptocurrencies, you need to understand all the above properties. Bitcoin as an irreversible, permissionless and pseudonymous method of payment as an attack on the control of governments and banks over monetary transactions of their citizens. There is no way to hinder someone from using Bitcoin; there is no way to prohibit someone from accepting Bitcoin and no way to undo a Bitcoin transaction.

Cryptocurrencies have attacked the scope of monetary policy since it is money with a controlled, limited supply and no central institution can change it, including a central bank or the government.

Cryptocurrencies are similar to digital gold: sound money free from political influence. It is a type of money with a promise of increasing its value over time and preserving it. The cryptocurrencies provide users with a comfortable and safe means of payment for cross-border transactions, and they are also anonymous and private enough to be used as means of payment in the black market, as well as in other outlawed activities. This is because it is hard to trace cryptocurrencies to a particular individual.

Although cryptocurrencies are popular for making payments, they are used as a means of storing value and speculation. They have brought about a fast-growing and dynamic market for speculators and investors. Exchanges such as Poloniex and OKcoin have provided platforms on which hundreds of cryptocurrencies can be traded. The daily trade volume for cryptocurrencies exceeds that of the major European exchanges.

Cryptocurrencies are characterized by extreme volatility. A coin may gain 10 or even 100 percent today and lose all of it the following day. For those who are lucky, the coin can grow up to 1000 percent in value within one or two weeks. So far, Bitcoin remains the most famous type of cryptocurrency, but it is good for you as an investor to watch how the other cryptocurrencies trend.

Chapter 2- Examples of Cryptocurrencies

There are several types of cryptocurrencies. Bitcoin is known as the first cryptocurrency running on blockchain technology. Other cryptocurrencies have sprouted, and they operate differently from Bitcoin. Let us discuss the various forms of cryptocurrency:

Bitcoin

This is the most famous type of cryptocurrency. It serves as the digital gold standard in the cryptocurrency world. It is used as a global means of payment and it's the de facto currency for cyber-crime like ransomware or darknet markets. Over 200,000 Bitcoin transactions are carried out on daily, and the price of the Bitcoin currency has risen from zero to about 650 dollars since the time it was discovered.

Bitcoin operates on the SHA-256 algorithm. It was discovered in 2009 by an anonymous person using the pseudonym, *Satoshi Nakamoto*. Due to the highly volatile nature of the Bitcoin cryptocurrency, it has become a choice of investment for people who need to benefit from speculation. However, due to the highly volatile nature of Bitcoin, individuals are avoiding investing in this cryptocurrency long-term. No one is willing to participate in a lengthy Bitcoin trade.

Currently, Bitcoin forms the most famous form of cryptocurrency since it's the oldest and media platforms are covering it on a daily basis. This is due to the innovative technical concept behind it and the rapid market changes. Bitcoin is used as the foundation of cryptocurrencies, which is why the prices of other cryptocurrencies are determined based on its price.

Once a Bitcoin payment has been done, it is impossible to reverse it. It is well known for the low number charged for Bitcoin transactions. Note that Bitcoin does not exist physically, but only balances are kept in a ledger stored in the cloud together with all the Bitcoin transactions that have been done. The verification of Bitcoin transactions consumes a high amount of computing power. There is no central bank or government that issues bitcoins, while individual bitcoins are not valuable as a commodity.

Bitcoin balances are stored using both private and public keys that are long strings joined via a mathematical encryption algorithm used when creating them. The public key is made available to the public and it may be compared to your bank account number. People use it when they need to send Bitcoins. For you to be able to authorize sending of bitcoins from your address, you must have the private key, hence it should be kept as a secret. The private key is similar to the PIN of your ATM card.

With Bitcoin, you can send and receive payments without having to provide details that identify you personally. Due to this, Bitcoin is referred as anonymous. This makes Bitcoin unique from other currencies offered by a government. When sending and receiving payments via Bitcoins, you can use a pseudonym. The pseudonym should be the address at which you will be receiving Bitcoin payments. This makes Bitcoin the best choice for individuals who want to remain anonymous when making and receiving online payments.

Bitcoin Transactions

Bitcoin transactions are sent from and received in Bitcoin wallets. They are signed digitally for security purposes. Every person is aware of every Bitcoin transaction, and one can trace back the history of the transaction to the point at which it was produced.

The funny thing about Bitcoins is that they don't exist anywhere, even on a hard drive. You will hear someone talk about having Bitcoins, but after looking at their Bitcoin address, you will find it holds no digital Bitcoins in a similar way that you may have pounds or dollars in your bank account. There is no single digital file or physical object that you can point to and say it's a Bitcoin.

Instead, you will only find records of transactions that have occurred between different addresses, together with balances that either increase or decrease. Each transaction that takes place is kept in a public ledger referred to as the block chain. For you to know the balance of a particular Bitcoin address, you have to look at the blockchain to reconstruct it.

Each Bitcoin transaction has three pieces of information. Suppose B sends some Bitcoins to A, the following pieces of information will be recorded:

1. The Input- this will record the address used to send Bitcoins to B. B had received the Bitcoins from a friend named E.

2. The Amount- the amount of Bitcoins B is sending to A.

3. The Output- the Bitcoin address of A.

How to Send Bitcoins

For one to be able to send Bitcoins, they must have two things, the private key and a Bitcoin address. The Bitcoin address is like a safe deposit box with a glass front. Everybody is aware of what it has inside, but only the private key can be used to unlock it and put things in or take them out.

When B needs to send some Bitcoins to A, he uses his private key to sign the message which contains the input, the amount and the output. B then sends out the Bitcoins from his Bitcoin wallet to the wider Bitcoin network. Bitcoin miners then verify the transaction, put it into the transaction block and finally solve it.

Your transactions must be verified by other miners, and this is why sometimes you may have to wait for them to finish mining. The Bitcoin blockchain has been designed in such a way that each block takes 10 minutes to mine.

Some merchants will make you wait for the transaction to be confirmed, meaning that it may take some time before you are allowed to download the digital goods or enjoy using the paid service.

However, some merchants will not make you wait for the transaction to be confirmed. They assume that you will not spend the Bitcoins somewhere else before the transaction is confirmed. This is mostly the case where the value of a transaction is low, meaning that the risk of fraud is minimal.

Bitcoins exist in the form of transactions, meaning that you may have different transactions all tied to one address. Maybe B had received different amounts of Bitcoins from different friends at separate times. The transactions will be stored as different transactions in B's wallet. For B to send Bitcoins to A, his wallet will combine the transactions whose value equals the amount of Bitcoins he needs to send to A.

There is a high chance that when B wants to send Bitcoins to A, there are no transactions whose value adds up to exactly that amount. The amount may be exceeded after combining the various transactions. B is not allowed to split the transactions into smaller amounts. One is only allowed to spend the whole output of a particular transaction. In such a case, B will send one of his incoming transactions, and the extra Bitcoins will be send to him in the form of change.

Suppose B wants to send 1.5 BTC to A. B had earlier on received 3 BTC from J. B can use the 3BTC received from J to pay A. In this case, J is the input, while A is the output. When sending the Bitcoins, the wallet will automatically create two outputs for his transaction. 1.5 BTC to A and 1.5 BTC to a new address created for B to hold change from A.

Where can one Buy Bitcoins?

There are various ways you can acquire or buy bitcoins. Let us discuss them:

Face-to-Face Trades

You can find a local seller and buy bitcoins from him/her. This is the best option for you if you live in a city; you don't need bank hassles or you may prefer anonymity.

You only have to visit a website such as LocalBitcoins and find a seller. You will then strike a deal on the site and make all the necessary arrangements. The good thing with the site is that it provides both parties with escrow protection, which means that they will be protected.

However, you must be careful when meeting a local bitcoin seller. Avoid meeting in private places as this is not good for your security. You can also visit a website such as Meetup.com and check whether Bitcoin meetings are held in your city. You can learn a lot about Bitcoin from such a group.

From Bitcoin ATMs

Bitcoin ATMs allow one to exchange bitcoins n compatible wallets for cash. However, these ATMs are only available in a number of cities, but they do provide one with an alternative for withdrawing money by use of an exchange. Also, most online wallets and exchanges do not deal with cash directly. Most Bitcoin ATMs are from companies such as Genesis Coin, BitAccess, Lamassu, CoinOutlet and Robocoin.

Investment Trust

You may not have an interest in buying and keeping huge amounts of bitcoins. In such a case, you can choose to use an investment trust. A good example of an investment trust is Winklevoss ETF and Bitcoin Investment Trust (BIT). The trust invests solely in bitcoins and it uses a modern protocol to keep the bitcoins safely on behalf of shareholders.

To buy bitcoins, you should go through the following steps:

1. Create a Bitcoin Wallet

   To be able to buy Bitcoins, you must have a Bitcoin wallet. You can choose from the various types of wallets discussed earlier. You can download the Bitcoin wallet from a website such as Blockchain.info or download the wallet to your mobile device. The process of setting up a Bitcoin wallet should be easy, and it will not take long to complete.

2. Buy Bitcoins

   After preparing the wallet, you can use traditional means such as a credit card, debit card or a bank transfer to buy the Bitcoins from an exchange such as Coinbase. After a successful payment, the Bitcoins will be transferred to your wallet. The payment method to be used is determined by your location and the exchange from wich you choose to buy Bitcoins.

Bitcoin Wallets

Bitcoin wallets provide us with a place to store bitcoins. There are various types of wallets in which one can store his or her bitcoins:

1. Desktop Wallets

   These are the wallets that are stored on a personal computer, and they can only be accessed with unique security keys kept on the same computer. They offer a number of advantages compared to online wallets in that they are not much exposed to the public, meaning they are less vulnerable to hackers and scammers. Due to the fact that your security keys are less exposed, your wallet remains safe. However, desktop wallets can still be hacked into in case the computer gets infected with a malware designed to steal bitcoins and root out keys.

An example of a desktop wallet is MultiBit which runs on Linux, Windows and Mac OS X. Hive is also a desktop wallet that runs solely on OS X, and it has some additional features including an app store that can connect you to Bitcoin services directly. Armory is another example of a desktop wallet, designed with security in mind. DarkWallet was designed to enhance anonymity, and it uses a lightweight browser plugin to offer services such as coin mixing, whereby the user's coins are exchanged for others so that people cannot track them.

2. Paper Wallet

Paper wallets provides Bitcoin users with a secure way of storing bitcoins, but the users are required to possess adequate knowledge about how digital currencies operate. Paper wallets are generated online using dedicated websites, or even offline for greater security. Paper wallets do not occupy much space, making it easy for one to store them, and they offer a high level of anonymity. Paper wallets are just a Bitcoin seed that has been written on a piece of paper.

There are numerous websites that offer paper Bitcoin wallet services. On the website, you can generate a Bitcoin address and the website will create an image with two QR codes, one being the public address through which you are able to receive bitcoins, and the other being a private address that can be used to authorize the transfer of bitcoins.

When using a paper wallet, the private keys are not stored using digital means, meaning that they are not prone to cyber-attacks common when using other types of Bitcoin wallets.

Note that with paper wallets, there is no way for you to know when money has arrived. Users have to rely on third-party blockchain explorers who can lie and even spy on them.

3. Ledger USB Wallet

   This type of USB wallet relies on Smartcard security and it is sold at an affordable cost.

4. Online wallets

   In these types of wallets, your private keys are stored online, on a computer that is under the control of someone else. The computer is connected to the Internet. These services are available, and some of them are linked to desktops and mobile wallets, meaning that the addresses are replicated on several devices you own.

   The good thing with online wallets is that they can be accessed from anywhere, regardless of the type of device one may be using. However, if you don't implement them correctly, the organization that runs the website may become under the control of your keys, meaning that you will lose control over your bitcoins. This can be risky, especially if you accumulate huge amounts of bitcoins.

Coinbase is an integrated wallet/bitcoin exchange with an online wallet operating worldwide. Users from the Europe and the U.S can buy bitcoins via this exchange.

Circle provides users from all over the world with a way to buy, store and send bitcoins. It only allows its US users to link their bank accounts and be able to deposit funds, but users from the other countries are allowed to use their credit and debit cards.

Blockchain provides you with a popular online wallet known as Strongcoin that provides a hybrid wallet that allows you to encrypt the keys for your private address before you can send them to the servers. The encryption process is normally done on the browser.

Trading your Bitcoins

If you have bitcoins, it is possible to trade them by selling them. There are a number of platforms on which you can sell your bitcoins. Other than on platforms, there are various other ways by which you can trade bitcoins.

LocalBitcoins

This site provides you with a website where you can advertise yourself as a Bitcoin seller to a wide audience. The website allows its users to rate one another, meaning that you are able to assess the trustworthiness of a trader. Once you get a reliable reputation, you will be in a position to sell with a premium attached to the Bitcoin price. Here, you are not required to verify your identity in the same way as on other websites.

LocalBitcoins also provides escrow protection services, but these are only offered for online transactions, not for in-person transfers. If someone asks for escrow protection for a face-to-face transaction, you don't have to comply.

Direct Sale

This can be the easiest way to sell your Bitcoins. You will only have to scan a QR code on the phone of another individual then accept cash-in-hand, which is a very easy process.

The process even becomes simpler if you have relative and friends who need to buy Bitcoins. You only have to send Bitcoins to their addresses, then you collect cash from them. However, it would be good to agree with your buyer on the rate that works for both of you. Your agreement can be based on what we have on a famous Bitcoin exchange, or CoinDesk Bitcoin Price Index. However, some sellers will choose to apply a particular percentage on the top of such rates as an anonymity/convenience premium or to help them cover costs. A mobile app can also be used for the calculation of prices. Examples of such apps include the BTCreport and Zeroblock. It will also be good for you to stay updated about fluctuations in prices. The prices will normally vary from one country to another, determined by the difficulty of getting Bitcoins using the local currency of the country. There are several Bitcoin meetups that take place across the world in which people normally buy and sell Bitcoins. You should take the necessary security measures when carrying huge amounts of cash to meet an individual with whom you need to trade.

You can advertise yourself as a Bitcoin seller. You can successfully do this on a website such as LocalBitcoins. On this website, you can rate each other, so it will be important for you to maintain your trustworthiness. After attaining a reliable reputation, it will be possible to make a sale with a premium attached. Here, you will not be expected to prove your identity as on the other websites.

On LocalBitcoins, escrow transactions are supported, but they can only be used for online transactions and not for face-to-face deals. If someone asks for escrow while transacting face-to-face, you don't have to agree.

Online Platforms

You can sell your bitcoins through online means. Here are ways through which you can do this:

1. Direct trades

   This involves a direct trade with another individual, and an intermediary who facilitates the connection. Examples of websites offering such a selling structure include BitBargain and Bittylicious in the UK and LocalBitcoins and Coinbase in the U.S.

   These websites require you to register as a seller. The registration process involves verification of your identity. After a successful registration, you will be able to create and post an offer, stating that you are in need of selling Bitcoins. The website will then notify you any time a buyer is found. You will interact with the seller, but all the trades will be completed on the website.

   When selling Bitcoins on Bittylicious and BitBargain UK, you must go through a long process, requiring patience. However, BitBargain UK offers very good support. If you have an account with a U.S bank, it is recommended that you use Circle or Coinbase which are very simple to use.

2. Exchange trades

You can also sell Bitcoins after registering with an online exchange. Such exchanges expect you to verify your identity, but you will not be expected to do much work when it comes to organizing the sale.

The exchanges act as an intermediary holding the funds for each participant. You are expected to place a sell order which states the volume or amount and the type of currency you need to sell, for example, Bitcoin. You will also be required to state the price per unit.

Once a buyer posts a buy order that matches your sale order, the exchange will complete the trade on your behalf. The currency will at the same time be credited to your account.

This process is easy, but it is associated with a disadvantage. If you are selling your bitcoins for fiat currencies, you will be expected to transfer the funds to your bank account. Sometimes, the exchange may be facing problems with the bank or liquidity problems. In such a case, it can take a long time for the funds to reflect in your bank account. This explains the need to do a research when choosing an exchange before you can commit your funds.

It is possible to use a pure cryptocurrency exchange to convert your Bitcoins to other forms of cryptocurrencies. However, this is not

common as people always need to convert
cryptocurrencies to fiat currencies. However,
you may need to buy something from a
merchant who accepts other forms of
cryptocurrencies besides Bitcoins. A good
example is the Bitcoin Shop which accepts
Dogeoin and Litecoin too.

When using some exchanges, you may be
required to pay a fee. To know the fees charged
by different cryptocurrency markets, you can
use Bitcoin Charts or visit CoinCompare and
you will be updated.

Exchanges also impose a limitation on the
amount of money you can store on the
exchange. This changes with time. However, it
is not a good idea to store all the coins you have
on an exchange if you are only speculating that
the price will rise. It would be good for you to

take responsibility for your funds and store any extra Bitcoins not currently needed in your own device such as offline storage.

3. Peer-to-peer marketing places

    With the rise in the popularity of Bitcoin, new websites have been developed that help two groups of people with specific and complimentary needs. Examples of such websites include Purse and Brawler.

    The first group is made up of individuals who need to use Bitcoins to buy goods from a website that does not accept payment via digital currencies directly. The second group is made up of individuals who need to buy Bitcoins using their credit or debit cards. Such marketplaces bring together individuals who have matching requirements to sell Bitcoins and to provide discounted goods and services.

The marketplace can be seen as an intermediary since it provides Bitcoin users with a Bitcoin wallet, and a platform and escrow for their transactions.

Bitcoin Mining

Bitcoin mining is the process that brings bitcoins into circulation. Without this process, we cannot have bitcoins in circulation. The Bitcoin mining process involves cryptographic puzzles requiring a high computation power that consumes a lot of electricity.

Whenever the government wants to have more money in circulation, they just print more paper money. This is then distributed throughout the country. In Bitcoin, there is no central government that can do this. This is why miners are expected to solve mathematical problems for which they are in turn rewarded with Bitcoins. It is a great way of creating the currency to allow many people to mine. Note that the reward is given to the first person who solves the cryptographic puzzle.

The Bitcoin mining process has been designed to be computationally intensive. This is in a bid to ensure that the number of blocks mined each day remains steady. For a block to be considered valid, it must have proof-of-work. The other Bitcoin miners must verify the this every time they receive the block. Bitcoin makes use of the hashcash proof-of-work function.

The goal of mining is to allow Bitcoin to make Bitcoin nodes reach a tamper-resistant and secure consensus. It is also a good way of bringing back bitcoins into the system as the miners are paid in Bitcoins and they receive a subsidy of coins that have been created. This is also a good way of motivating the miners to secure the system.

Proof-of-Work

A proof-of-work is simply a piece of data that is difficult to produce to satisfy a particular set of requirements. The production of a proof-of-work may be a random process with a low probability, meaning that a lot of trial and error will be needed for the miner to generate a valid proof-of-work. Bitcoin makes use of Hashcash proof-of-work.

Block Reward

A block reward are bitcoins that a miner earns after successfully discovering a new block. As stated earlier, this is normally 25 bitcoins. However, this value halves after mining of 210,000 blocks. Also, the miner is also paid from the fees sent by the users who send transactions. The fee is paid as an incentive for a miner to add a transaction to their block. With time, the percentage of this fee will become significant.

Network Difficulty Problem

This is the measure of how hard or difficult it is for one to discover a new Bitcoin block compared to how easy the process can be. This must be recalculated after each 2016 blocks to some value in such a way that the past 2016 should have been generated in two weeks if everyone were mining at that difficulty. On average, this yields one block per 10 minutes.

As more miners join the network, the difficulty goes up. If the rate at which the blocks are generated increases, the difficulty also increases to compensate, and the rate of block generation goes down. Any blocks generated by malicious miners on the network will not meet the required difficulty target and the miners will be able to identify and reject them. This means the blocks will be worthless.

Computationally-Difficult Problem

Mining a Bitcoin block is difficult since the SHA-256 hash of the block's header has to be lower than or equal to the target for the network to accept the block. For the miner to get a hash of a block that begins with the required number of zeroes, they must go through a number of trials while changing the nonce. For a new hash to be generated in each iteration, the value of the nonce must be incremented.

Mining Hardware

The Bitcoin mining process requires a set of hardware or tools that facilitate the mining process. Initially, Bitcoin mining required the use of very simple hardware. Currently, more powerful hardware is required for mining Bitcoins. Below are the hardware you should have to mine Bitcoin:

1. CPU

Initially, one could only mine Bitcoins using the CPU, and the original Satoshi client was commonly used. However, the need to earn more Bitcoins and secure the network has made miners discover many new fonts which has made CPU mining futile. You can use your laptop for mining and earn no coins in a decade.

2. GPU

It was later discovered that the use of a graphics card was a much more efficient way of Bitcoin mining. CPU mining was replaced by GPU mining (Graphical Processing Unit). This increased the rate of Bitcoin mining by 50X to 100X, and the power consumption also reduced. It is true that any modern GPU is suitable for mining, but the AMD line GPU has been found to be the most suitable GPU for Bitcoin mining.

3. ASIC

ASIC (Application Specific Integrated Circuit) is the current technology for Bitcoin mining. An ASIC is simply a chip designed and developed for doing one task only. Note that the ASIC cannot be used to perform any other task other than the one it has been designed to do. If it has been designed to mine Bitcoins, it can only be used to mine Bitcoins. This has made it increase the mining power up to 100X and reduce the power consumption compared to previous technologies. There are chances that this technology will mark the end of disruptive mining technology. This is because there is nothing at the moment nor in the near future to replace ASIC. A refinement will be made to ASIC products to improve their efficiency, but there is nothing expected to increase the hashing power by 50X or 100X, or reduce the power consumption by 7X. The ability of this product to consume less power makes it popular for use in mining Bitcoins. It is believed that if you have purchased an ASIC device for Bitcoin mining today, it will still be used in mining Bitcoins two years in the future, provided the cost of electricity doesn't exceed the output. The exchange rate also determines the amount of profit earned from mining, but mining devices that are efficient in terms of power consumption are the best for more profitability.

4. FPGA

As with the CPU to GPU transition, the technology for Bitcoin has also advanced to the FPGA (Field Programmable Gate Array). This is a special hardware developed solely for Bitcoin mining. This hardware did not bring about a huge increase in processing power like the GPU, but it has brought a huge benefit to Bitcoin mining by reducing power consumption 5X.

Ethereum

This is another type of cryptocurrency that runs on blockchain technology. However, it is more than just a cryptocurrency. Ethereum is a blockchain platform that is decentralized and runs smart contracts. Smart contracts are simply computer codes that can facilitate the exchange of content, money, shares, property or anything with value.

Ethereum allows developers to create operations on the blockchain that run in the way they have been programmed without the possibility of downtime, censorship, fraud or even third-party interference.

Ethereum is the first world's blockchain supercomputer fueled by a cryptocurrency known as *Ether*. Ether is a tradable cryptocurrency and its market cap currently stands at over $34 billion. App developers also use Ether when paying for the transaction fees as well as services offered on the Ethereum network. The value of Ether has increased rapidly, which is why most investors are rushing to it. A maximum of 18 million Ether is supplied every year and there are over 95.7 million Ether tokens currently in circulation.

Ethereum platform allows application developers to develop and deploy decentralized applications. Just like the Bitcoin blockchain, Ethereum is a public blockchain network that is distributed. However, Bitcoin and Ethereum differ in terms of purpose and capability. Bitcoin provides one of the applications of blockchain technology, that is, a peer-to-peer electronic cash system that can be used for online Bitcoin payments. Bitcoin blockchain focusses on tracking the ownership of digital currency, that is, bitcoins, but the focus of the Ethereum blockchain is to run the code for any decentralized application.

Instead of mining as happens in Bitcoin, in Ethereum, the miners work to earn Ether, the crypto currency that fuels the Ethereum network.

Smart Contracts

These are just computer codes that facilitate various processes on the Ethereum blockchain. The code is created in such a way that it will run automatically once a number of conditions are met. Note that smart contracts run as programmed by the developer. This means that there is no possibility of fraud, censorship, downtime or interference by third parties.

It is a fact that all blockchains are capable of processing code, but most of them are limited. This is not the case with Ethereum. Instead of giving users a limited set of operations, Ethereum allows developers to create any kind of operation they need to use. This is an indication that the developers are capable of developing applications that can do what we have not seen so far.

Ethereum Virtual Machine

Before Ethereum was created, a very limited set of operations could be performed with blockchain technology. Bitcoin as well as the other cryptocurrencies were, for example, to be used as peer-to-peer cryptocurrencies.

With time, the developers were facing a problem. The solution was to either expand the functions provided by Bitcoin and other cryptocurrencies, which is a time-consuming and complicated process, or create a new blockchain as well as platform. This led to Vitalik Buterin, the developer of Ethereum, who came up with a new approach.

The Ethereum Virtual Machine (EVM) is the core innovation of Ethereum, a Turing software that runs on the Ethereum network. With the EVM, one can run any program despite the programming language, provided there is memory and time. The Ethereum Virtual Machine has made the process of creating blockchain applications as simple as it could ever be. Instead of having to develop some new blockchain for every application, it is now possible to develop thousands of applications on a similar platform.

The Ether

The goal of Ethereum is to function as both a decentralized app store as well as a decentralized Internet and this leads to the support of a Dapp (decentralized application).

Although there is no one who can claim to own Ethereum, the system is not available for free. The network is in need of Ether, a unique piece of code used to pay for the computational resources needed to run the program or application.

Just like Bitcoin, Ether is a digital bearer asset similar to security such as a bond that has been issued in a physical form. In the same way as cash, a third party is not needed to approve or process a transaction. However, instead of operating like a digital currency or payment, the Ether provides fuel to the decentralized apps (Dapps) that run on the network. They work in the same way that tokens power the user experience.

Suppose you have a decentralized online notebook. For you to post, modify or delete the note, you are expected to pay a transaction fee in the form of Ether so that the network may process the change. This explains why Ether has sometimes been known as "digital oil". The fee charged on the Ethereum network is based on the amount of gas required to complete an action. Each action requires an amount of gas to run, and the amount of gas needed is determined by the amount of computation power you need as well as the amount of time required to complete the action.

The economy of Ether has a set of open-ended rules. In Bitcoin, there are only 21 million bitcoins. However, there is no such limitation in ether. Of all the existing Ether, 60m of it was purchased in 2014 by users taking part in a crowdfunding campaign. 12m of the Ether went to Ethereum Foundation, a group of developers and researchers working on underlying technology. After each 12 seconds, 5 Ethers are allotted to the miners on the network whose work is to verify transactions.

At most, eighteen million Ether are mined each year. Each 12 seconds, five Ethers are created once a miner has discovered a block or transactions in a bundle. Currently, no one knows the total amount of Ether, and the rate at which it is created will not be clear until after Ethereum has moved to new proof-of-stake algorithm. The rules governing the creation of Ether will also change, and the subsidy earned from mining Ether may be reduced.

What is the use of Ethereum?

Ethereum can be used for the development of decentralized applications (Dapps). A Dapp helps its users perform a particular task. Bitcoin is an example of a Dapp that provides its users with a peer-to-peer electronic cash system that facilitates online Bitcoin payments. Since Dapps are made to run on the blockchain, there is no single individual or authority controlling them.

Centralized services can be decentralized using Ethereum. This means that we can use Ethereum to decentralize voting systems, banking systems, regulatory compliance, title registries etc. We can also use Ethereum in building Decentralized Autonomous Organizations (DAOs). This is a decentralized autonomous organization without a single leader. The DAOs are executed by programming the code on a collection of smart contracts written on Ethereum blockchain. The code has been designed to replace the structure and rules of traditional organization so that the need for people and a centralized control is eliminated. The DAO is owned by anyone who purchases tokens, and these tokens are the contributions that gives one voting rights.

Ethereum Wallets

Ethereum wallets provide a secure way of storing Ether. The wallet is associated with a private key, which when lost, causes all the Ether in the wallet to be lost. There are no intermediaries required to approve the transactions, but this also means that there is no one to contact to recover the secret key in case it is lost. There are various types of wallets in which you can store your Ether. The choice of wallet depends on security and convenience. However, note that the higher the convenience of accessing the wallet, the less secure it is:

Desktop Wallets

These are wallets that run on a laptop or PC. You can download an Ethereum client, which is a copy of a whole Ethereum blockchain. Note that Ethereum clients are of different types since they are developed in different programming languages. The clients also differ in terms of performance. The process may take a number of days and it increases with the growth of Ethereum. The wallet should be kept in sync with the latest blockchain transactions.

Mobile Wallets

Light clients require less data to download and connect to the network for making transactions. This makes them suitable for use by mobile clients. While they are convenient, they are not very safe for Ether storage. With full Ethereum clients, one has a more secure way of receiving transactions since there is no need to trust the nodes or miners to send accurate information, since they themselves validate the transactions.

The storage of private keys on a device that has been detached from the Internet (a process called "cold storage") is the best way of storing ether since it is very hard to hack. However, the process is hard to use especially in cases where the Ether has been stored on a smartphone or computer that has been connected to the Internet.

Hardware Wallets

These are small wallets and are the best option for the storage of Ether. It is possible to detach hardware wallets from the Internet, and they can even sign Ether transactions without the need of being online.

However, since hardware wallets function like a deposit box, they are not a good option for use if you will need to use Ether frequently or when travelling.

Paper Wallets

This is another cold storage option that involves writing the private key on a piece of paper or printing it, then locking it in a secure place such as a deposit box. You can use online tools to generate the key pairs directly on your computer, but the servers of the website are not secure as the keys can be stolen if the website is hacked.

You can also use the command line to generate the keys, but you should have the right cryptographic packages installed for the language you prefer. Also, note that if the private key is lost, it will be lost for good. This means that you should make several copies of the private key and keep them in different secure locations so that if one is lost or damaged, you use the other.

Buying Ether

The process of buying Ether is determined by the country you are in and the currency you have. You must find someone with Ether who needs to trade it for another currency. You can find the person online or in person. People living in cities such as Toronto and New York are lucky as there are ether meet ups at which you can get someone to sell Ether. However, this option is not available for those living in less populated cities. In such a case, you can rely on an exchange from where you will exchange your currency for Ether. In most exchanges, you are allowed to buy Ether with Bitcoins or US dollars. Typically, you have to go through a sign-up process, but be sure no personal details will be asked.

To buy using another currency, you may be required to go through a number of steps. Bitcoin forms the most popular cryptocurrency in the world, hence people want you to use it when trading with them. This means that if you have rubbles and you need to purchase Ether, you should first purchase Bitcoins from an exchange, then use them to purchase the Ether. After getting your Ether, you will be able to send it directly to another person, known as peer-to-peer, and a small transaction fee will be charged and be paid to the miners on the Ethereum network.

Up to this point, you have seen a lot of similarities between Bitcoin and Ether. However, the two have different applications. With Ether, you can create smart contracts to be executed anytime without your interference or even relying on third parties. You can use bundles of the smart contracts to create decentralized applications.

Ethereum wallets are also identified via private and public keys, just like Bitcoin wallets. The keys are represented using a sequence of letters and numbers, and they are linked together through means of cryptography. You can share the public key with others so that they know where to send money. To be able to receive Ether, you need a public address, a string of letters and numbers obtained from the public key you have, and then people will be able to send Ether to you.

To be able to spend Ether, you must sign the transaction using your private key. This can be seen as the same as the PIN you use to unlock your funds when using an ATM card. The good thing with Bitcoin and Ethereum is that users are allowed to generate an identification number for their funds at any time. This means that they are not required to wait for their account to be approved in the same way that it is done in banks.

Mining Ethereum

The goal of mining Ethereum is to generate Ether in a way that does not require any central issuer. Ethereum tokens are generated through the mining process, and one earns 5 Ethers for every mined block. There is a need for proper record keeping on the Ethereum network. Mining ensures it is achieved, and the miners must come to a consensus in a bid to ensure there is no fraud.

The Ethereum mining process is similar to the Bitcoin mining process. Miners must use their computers to guess answers to puzzles until one of them gets it right. The unique header metadata of the block (which includes the timestamp and software version) is run through a hash function which, in turn, returns a fixed-length sequence of numbers and letters. Only the "nonce" value is changed so that we get a different hash value.

The miner is awarded after finding a hash that matches the current target. The award is normally in the form of Ether, after which the new block is broadcast to each node on the network so that they can validate and add it to their own ledger. If miner B, for example, finds the target hash, then miner A will stop working on it and begin to work on the next block.

It is hard for miners to cheat in Ethereum mining. There is no way you can fake the work to find the correct answer for the puzzle. This is why the method of solving the puzzle is known as *proof-of-work*. The process of verifying the hash takes a very short time.

However, note that the supply of Ether is not infinite. Control of the amount of Ether on the network was decided in a 2014 presale. The amount of Ether issues each year cannot exceed 18 million. This mechanism is employed to reduce on inflation.

Each block should have a proof-of-work of a particular difficulty to be validated into a consensus. The algorithm responsible for validation of the blocks is known as Ethash. It is responsible for taking the nonce input and mapping it to a result below a threshold specified as a way of controlling the difficulty. If the difficulty is manipulated, the miner will be able to control the amount of time required to find a new block.

The difficulty must be manipulated frequently to ensure that the network produces only one block after every 12 seconds. You can mine Ethereum from the comfort of your home. Knowledge of how to write scripts and use the command prompt is needed. The process becomes much easier once it has been broken down into manageable steps.

A lot of electricity is consumed during Ethereum mining. However, in return, if the mining process is done efficiently, one can generate much income. There are Ethereum calculators available to calculate the profits in Ethereum mining. You don't have to get worked up as you will earn a profit at the end of the process.

Ethereum Mining Hardware

To mine Ethereum, you can even use your laptop provided it has a graphics card and a RAM of 2 GB. Mining with a CPU (Central Processing Unit) can be frustrating. It can take too much time and the profits may be small due to the huge costs involved. GPUs offer performance that is 200X faster than CPUs, making them the best for mining Ether. AMD cards better compared to the Nvidia cards. Mining calculators will help you know the amount of Ether you earn compared to the amount of electricity you consume so you can determine whether you will end up with a profit or a loss.

Ethereum Mining Software

Once you have chosen the mining hardware, the next step is to install the mining software. The miner should begin by installing the client so they can connect to the network. If you are a programmer and like using the command prompt, you can install "Geth" which will provide you with an Ethereum node written in the Go scripting language.

Begin by downloading the Geth, choosing the right version based on the operating system you are using, unzip then run it. Note that Geth comes in versions for Windows, Linux and Mac OS. After the software has been installed, your node will be able to talk to the other nodes and connect to the Ethereum network. Other than the ability to mine Ether, you will be provided with a user interface through which you can deploy smart contracts and send transactions via the command line.

Ethminer

To be able to mine real Ether, you should install a real mining software. At this point, you have downloaded the client and it is part of the network, so you can now download Ethminer. Make sure you download the right one based on the operating system you are running. After it has been installed, your node will be tasked with the responsibility of securing your network.

Mining Pools

Mining Ether on your own might be tough. Miners usually combine their mining power into "mining pools" to increase their chances of solving cryptographic puzzles and earning Ether. The profits earned from such a mining process are shared on the basis of the amount of power one has contributed.

There are a number of factors involved when joining a mining pool. Every pool may not be available forever, and the power of computation of each pool keeps on changing, so a number of factors should be considered when choosing a pool to join. Note that mining pools do not have same payout structures.

To join a mining pool, you will be taken through a signup process on a website before you are allowed to join a pool and begin mining Ether. Again, it would be good for you to stay updated with what is current in the market as new Ethereum mining tools are discovered on a yearly basis. Ensure that your hard disk has enough space, probably around 30GB. This is enough for the blockchain.

Just like Bitcoin, Ethereum relies on the Proof of Work (PoW) system. It involves solving of complex equations, and miners must clear or meet this so that their blocks can be added to the blockchain. The system has an impact on the environment and it consumes too much electricity. However, by use of the Dagger Hashimoto algorithm, individuals can mine Ethereum using their home computers incurring a minimal expenditure. However, there are plans for the process of mining Ethereum to be replaced completely by a mechanism known as Proof of Stake, and a consensus algorithm will be powering this. The Ethereum network is simply a string of connections maintained by computers, with an undeniable impact and good profit.

Litecoin

Litecoin was developed in 2009 by an MIT graduate and Google engineer. It relies on an open source global network not under the control of a centralized authority. In Litecoin, script is used as the proof-of-work, and it can be decrypted by use of CPUs of consumer grade. The rate at which blocks are generated in Litecoin is faster compared to the rate in Bitcoin. This means that Litecoin transactions can be verified and confirmed faster compared to Bitcoin.

Litecoin Mining

The process of mining litecoin is spread across a network of miners. The miners have to assemble all the new transactions which appear on the Litecoin network into large bundles known as *blocks*, and these blocks are make a record of all the transactions that have made to give a *blockchain.*

To ensure that there is only one blockchain, Litecoin makes it hard to mine blocks. Instead of the miner only making the block available, a cryptographic hash for the block has to be produced that must meet a specified criteria; and to find this, you have to try many times until you are lucky and get the right one. This process is referred to as *hashing.* After a miner has successfully created a block, they in turn earn 25 freshly minted Litecoins as the reward.

After a few days, the difficulty of this criteria for the hash will have to be adjusted depending on the frequency with which blocks are appearing, and there is a lot of competition, the miners will have to do more work to find the blocks. This is known as *networkdifficulty,* and it is equal to all of the miners with a value of 688,270.

Mining Litecoin can be profitable, but a number of conditions do apply. The profits earned by mining with ASICs is higher, but one may not make profits when mining Litecoin with CPUs and GPUs. This is because the costs will exceed the profits, even when the electricity is provided for free.

Mining Pools

It is always hard to find a block. Even when you are using very powerful hardware, it may take you months or even years to find a block. This has led to the invention of mining pools, whereby miners come together to share processing power and mine Litecoins faster. Pool users usually earn shares after submitting valid proofs-of-work, and the payment is made based on the amount of effort one puts out in finding a block.

There are two reward systems commonly used in rewarding Litecoin miners that include the following:

1. Pay per Share- in this system, users are not rewarded on the number of blocks the pool finds, but rather depending on the number of blocks that the pool was expected to find based on the amount of work done by users. The pool will pay a fixed amount of Litecoins for every valid share the users submit, employing mathematical laws of probability. With this system, miners can enjoy steady payouts and a minimal variance, and there is no need to wait for the blocks to be confirmed. However, the system has a disadvantage in that the pool operator has the risk of any bad luck that may occur.

2. Proportional systems are round-based: in this case, the pool will wait until one of the users

finds a block, and the reward will be distributed amongst the users. This is done according to the number of shares each user submits.

You must be wise when choosing a mining pool, and you have to consider a number of factors including user support, reliability, reputability and its features.

Mining Software

The ASIC mining hardware usually comes with the mining software installed, and little or no configuration is needed. However, you may be in in need of doing CPU mining, maybe for experimental purposes. In such a case, you will have to download the Pooler's cpuminer. In the case of GPU mining, it is hard to setup and is not efficient compared to CPU and ASIC mining. This means that GPU mining is a bad idea unless you are doing it for research purposes. Begin by downloading the cpuminer software, then extract it on your computer. It is good to create a folder for the cpuminer on the desktop.

The GPU Miner

Although mining Litecoin with GPU is not recommended, you can still go for it. If this is the case, you must download the cgminer program from the developer's website. In case you are using Mac OS, download its unofficial binaries. Our assumption in this case is that you will be mining the script currency.

Once the software has been downloaded, extract it to a directory that can be found easily, such as "c:\cgminer\". Update your graphic drivers before you make the next step.

Press the Windows key together with the R key, then type "cmd" and hit the enter key. The command terminal will be opened. By use of the "cd" command, navigate to the directory where you have kept the zip file for cgminer. Type the command "cgminer.exe –n ". All the recognized devices on your system will be listed. If the system detects your graphics card, you will be lucky. In case this does not happen, search and follow all the steps necessary to set the specifics of the graphics cards.

How to buy Litecoin

Litecoin cryptocurrency was developed to be lightweight and more abundant compared to Bitcoin. An easy way of buying Litecoins is by using Bitcoins. To most users, this is the cheapest and easiest approach.

There are a number of exchanges from which individuals with Bitcoins can purchase Litecoins. Examples include BTC-e, Kraken, Cryptsy among others. Currently, Litecoin is facing a challenge in that no exchanges are ready and willing to deal with it.

There are currently about two dozen Litecoin exchanges, but most only allow for BTC/LTC exchanges; this has made the process of buying cumbersome.

Exchanges such as Bitfinex, BTC-E, Kraken and Crypto-Trade usually sell Litecoins for rubles, dollars and euros, but the availability is determined by your location.

The main advantage of buying Litecoins through Bitcoin is speed. Theoretically, this should only take minutes, but international wire transfers may take days to clear while incurring additional costs. Due to the limited availability of Litecoin exchanges, investors are forced to rely on international transfers.

The alternative s buying Bitcoins locally. This way, you will be able to get your Litecoin sooner and enjoy a better price when converting it, provided its value of keeps on going up. However, if you are limited to a local market only, you may end up paying more for the Litecoin.

Most exchanges provide their users with online Litecoin wallets. It is a fact that offline cold wallets are the best for many users due to their security. However, Litecoin comes with a in-built encryption that can help you protect or secure your wallet in just a few clicks.

There are few choices for the Litecoin wallet compared to those for the Bitcoin wallet. It is good to read the terms of service for a wallet before you begin to use it. Some wallets will charge the users for transactions as well as for plain storage. If you are in need of a wallet for longer-term cold storage, you can setup a Litecoin paper wallet. You can also get "paper wallet" cards with a quality similar to a credit card.

Zcash

Zcash is a type of cryptocurrency that runs on a decentralized blockchain capable of providing anonymity to users and their transactions. Zcash and Bitcoin as cryptocurrencies have a number of similarities such as being open-source, but there is a major difference in the level of fungibility and privacy provided by each. Zcash provides a high level of fungibility by allowing users to remain completely anonymous.

Zcash was founded in October 2016 by Zooko Wilcox-O'Hearn with the goal of providing a cryptocurrency that provides users with a financial system at the level of privacy they need. Bitcoin can be seen as the pioneer of open-source financial systems. Zcash implements this, but with privacy and fungibility under consideration. Fungibility refers to the ease with which a particular commodity can be substituted for another. This is a very important property in the cryptocurrency world since it ensures that the coin of a particular user is as important as the coin of the other user. Bitcoin provides an open ledger system, while Zcash provides an encrypted open ledger. This is an indication that although all the transactions are added to the blockchain, only the users with the necessary access permissions will be allowed to view them.

In Zcash, Equihash is used as the encryption algorithm, an asymmetric and memory-hard PoW algorithm. This algorithm requires a large RAM so that it can bottleneck the generation of proofs and make the development of ASIC unfeasible just like Ethereum. Zcash is normally abbreaviated as ZEC. Although it is a new cryptocurrency, it operates similarly to Bitcoin and other cryptocurrencies. You can buy and sell ZEC on online exchanges such as Kraken and Poloniex.

In cryptocurrencies, users rely on the use of private and public keys. The public keys act as the identifier for users and a sender must know to be able to do the transfer. The private key gives the user access to his coins. With time, when several transactions have been made, the public address can be linked to the transactions, making it possible for any inquirer to know the holder of the public address. This is where fungibility comes in. If a product seller is able to track the previous transactions done by a client from the public address the buyer gives the seller, the seller can choose to reject payments from that buyer if his payment history doesn't match what he needs.

Zcash uses a cryptographic tool known as *Zero-Knowledge Proof* with which two parties are able to transact without having to reveal their public addresses to each other. It obfuscates the addresses of the users involved in the transaction as well as the amount, making the transaction untraceable. It becomes hard for one to trace the path between the sender and the receiver. This is not the case with other blockchains like Bitcoin in which the amount transferred between the sender and receiver is shown. This is how fungibility helps in Zcash.

There are a number of reasons why users will want to use such anonymous cryptocurrencies such as Zcash other than drug trafficking, gun smuggling and shady activities done on the dark web. A company may be in need of protecting its secret information from competitors, an individual with a chronic disease may need to hide it from the public when buying pills, an individual may need a legal service for a private reason such as bankruptcy, or an individual may be buying bedroom toys, etc.

Mining Zcash

Not everyone has access to a computer as well as the time and knowledge to start mining Zcash on their own. The graphical user interface developed so far to help in mining Zcash is not easy. To mine Zcash with CPU, you can use the Nicerhash miner, while if you need to mine Zcash with GPU, use claymore miner.

CPU Mining

We will use the Nicehash miner to mine the Zcash. Here are the steps:

1. Begin by downloading the Nicehash miner. Make sure you download the latest release of the software.
2. Next, extract your files within a .zip. To be able to use the software, you will must specify the

number of cores you have to get maximum performance. You can check the task manager. Note that there are two versions of NiceHash, with one allowing for payment through Bitcoins and another for payment through Zcash.

3. Next, open "**nheqminer_zcash" file.**

4. **To begin mining with the CPU, you will have to type or even paste the command given below and make any modifications needed:**

nheqminer_zcash.exe -l eu - u ZEC-ADDRESS -t 8

The "eu" should be replaced with the address of your mining pool found on the "Get Started" page of the pool, ZEC-ADDRESS with address of your Zcash wallet and the "-t 8" with the number of threads you need to use. For those using a NiceHash pool, feel free to use the –l option and specify your location, such as "eu" for Europe.

GPU Mining

You can use the Claymore miner to mine Zcash with GPU. Claymore software has a good reputation when it comes to optimization of miners. It is also good for improving the rate of hashing, which is why we are going to use this miner. The Genoil miner can only be used in pool mining and works only with AMD graphics cards. The miner charges a fee of 2.5%. However, the performance outweighs the fees charged.

Catalyst 15.12 helps ensure there is compatibility and a better performance. Different versions of the drivers will give you different results, and sometimes the miner fails to start up. In the case of multi-GPU systems, the size of the virtual memory in Windows should be set to at least 16GB. To access this, navigate through the following:

"Computer Properties / Advanced System Settings / Performance / Advanced / Virtual Memory"

Here are the steps:

1. Begin by downloading the Claymore Zcash miner.
2. Identify the latest version of the miner, then download it.
3. Next extract the files in a .zip.
4. Open the folder for "**Claymore's ZCash AMD GPU Miner v6.0 Beta**".

5. **In a text editor such as Notepad, open the "config.txt" file, then add the following configuration to it:**

GPU_FORCE_64BIT_PTR 0

GPU_MAX_HEAP_SIZE 100

GPU_USE_SYNC_OBJECTS 1

GPU_MAX_ALLOC_PERCENT 100

GPU_SINGLE_ALLOC_PERCENT 100

ZecMiner64.exe -zpool stratum.zcash.nicehash.com:3357 -allpools 1 -zwal t1RjQjDbPQ9Syp97DHFyzvgZhcjgLTMwhaq.YourWorkerName -zpsw x

The "**stratum.zcash.nicehash.com:3357**" **should be replaced by the server of your pool. The "t1RjQjDbPQ9Syp97DHFyzvgZhcjgLTMwhaq" should be replaced with the**

address of your wallet. You can also replace the work name as well as the password if you need to do so.

You will now see the process of mining Zcash begin. You only have to sit down and watch.

Ripple

This is a real-time global payment network that provides a certain instant and low-cost method for making international payments. With Ripple, banks and other financial institutions can make cross-border payments in real time while providing a high level of transparency at a low cost. The consensus ledger of Ripple does not need mining, contrary to what happens in Bitcoin and other cryptocurrencies. Since the structure of Ripple does not require mining, it minimizes the network latency and reduces computing power.

The Ripple blockchain was developed to address the need to keep money flowing freely. Banks and other financial institutions restricts the transfer of money by charging of fees and other means. Ripple is built on the decentralized digital currency approach set by Bitcoin and uses the Internet to do for money what it did for all other types of information.

OpenCoin is the company behind the development of Ripple. CEO, Chris Larsen, and CTO, Jed McCaleb, are the co-founders of OpenCoin. McCaleb had good knowledge of digital currency since he came from Mt. Gox, the company that does most of the world's Bitcoin trades. The other developers on the Ripple's team also had a Bitcoin background.

You may think that Ripple is a competitor to Bitcoin, but this is not the case. Instead, Ripple acts as a complement to Bitcoin. The Ripple network was designed and built to allow for a seamless transfer of various forms of currency, including euros, dollars, pounds, Bitcoins, yen, etc. It opens up many gateways for Bitcoin users and provides them with easy ways to bridge Bitcoin with the world of finance.

Other than providing Bitcoin with ways to connect to those using other types of currency, it promises an increased stability and expedited transactions. Since Ripple is a distributed network, there is no need to rely on a single company to secure and manage the transaction database. Also, there is no need to wait for block confirmations, and confirmations of transactions can quickly go through the network. Due to the use of peer-to-peer, the system does not have a central point of failure.

Other Types of Cryptocurrencies

The following are other types of cryptocurrencies used in the world:

1. Monero (XMR)

   Monero is a private, secure and untraceable currency. It was started in April 2014 and since then has attracted a large number of cryptocurrency enthusiasts. The development of Monero was based on donations from the community. It was developed with a great focus on scalability and decentralization, and it uses a special technique known as *ring signatures* to facilitate privacy. With the ring signatures technique, there are several cryptographic signatures with only one coming from a real participant. All the signatures seem to be valid, making it difficult to tell which one is real to isolate it. One of the great features of Monero is its perceived anonymity. Although it provides users with a very good privacy, it is geared towards being opaque. This feature is making it a popular type of cryptocurrency for use on the dark web, where Bitcoin is not much used.

2. Dash

Dash was originally referred to as *Darkcoin*, a type of more secretive Bitcoin. It provides its users with a higher level of anonymity since it runs on a decentralized mastercode network on which transactions are almost untraceable. It was released in January of 2014 and has since gained a very large following. Evan Dufield is the one behind its design and development and the cryptocurrency can be mined using either CPU or GPU. It was given the name, Dash, in March of 2015, which means Digital Cash; and it operates under ticker-DASH. However, there were no changes made to the cryptocurrency during its rebranding.

Dash relies on a two-tier architecture for powering its network. It also runs a Decentralized Autonomous Organization (DAO). The goal of Dash is to be the first privacy-centric cryptocurrency by providing fully encrypted transactions and anonymous block transactions. The aim of developing Dash was to solve the problems made during the development of Bitcoin. It is also intended to be faster and cheaper than Bitcoin. It is one of the few altcoins used by people for buying goods and services.

3. TRON

This cryptocurrency is expected to take on the Internet giants such as YouTube and Facebook for creative types. It is expected to decentralize the web so that artists, musicians and other users are able to share their materials with the world without having to rely on centralized services.

4. IOTA

   IOTA stands for Internet of Things Application. The cryptocurrency is expected to shape the future of connected devices just like the name implies. The idea behind its development is that with the increase in the number of devices connected to the Internet, from smart cars to iPhones, the number of micropayments will also increase.

5. NEM

   This is another project based on blockchain technology geared towards improving things such as payments and logistics. It tries to make itself unique by creating a customizable blockchain. It suits both beginners and experienced blockchain developers.

6. Stellar

   This has been implemented to work in the way that banks, people and payment networks move money.

Chapter 3- Cryptocurrencies vs. Fiat Money

Fiat money refers to money that the government has declared to be legal tender. The value of fiat money is determined by the forces of demand and supply rather than the material used to make the money.

A cryptocurrency on the other hand is a digital asset designed to be used as a medium of exchange. It relies on cryptocurrency to secure the transactions between users to control or regulate the creation of additional units of the currency.

Examples of fiat money include the US dollar, the euro, the Japanese yen, etc. Examples of cryptocurrencies include Ether, Bitcoin, Litecoin, etc.

Let us discuss the various ways in which the two differ:

Acquiring

Onecan acquire fiat money through various methods such as salaries, wages, the lottery, sales or investments. On the other hand, we can obtain cryptocurrencies via cryptocurrency exchanges, crypto mining, wages and salaries (very rare) and sales.

Where to use Them

Fiat currency can only be used within the borders of the issuing country. International reserve currencies such as the euro, dollar and the Japanese yen can also be used internationally as a reserve for settling international contracts and for exchanging for local currencies in other countries.

Cryptocurrencies can only be used online for payment of goods and services but to a lesser extent. Some mortar and brick businesses do access cryptocurrencies as a form of payment for services only.

Is there profit for holding it?

The value of fiat money suffers from inflation. As services and goods increase in price, the value of money goes down. The value of fiat money may also increase or decrease based on other currencies and macroeconomic factors. When using fiat money, interest payments are generated for users. Interest rates are normally set by the central bank in a bid to regulate inflation and the supply of money.

Naturally, cryptocurrency is deflationary, and its price is less influenced by the prices of goods and services. The increase or decrease in the price of cryptocurrency is determined by demand. Note that the supply of the cryptocurrency is always fixed. Cryptocurrency users are not liable to any interest payments since there is no central bank responsible for issuing it. The supply of a cryptocurrency is fixed, meaning that only market forces are responsible for any phenomenon associated with its value.

Safety

It is possible to counterfeit fiat money, but this is difficult. Double spending is avoided by physical possession of the notes and coins. Coins and bills have different seals and holograms as well as other features hard to counterfeit.

Cryptocurrencies are secured via cryptography, which makes it nearly impossible to counterfeit them. Cryptocurrencies are simply pieces of information, hence they are easy to copy or reproduce. Double spending is prevented via transaction logs. Each transaction is made public to all nodes in the blockchain. It becomes easy to view the legitimacy of a transaction or block. Fake blocks added to the blockchain are easily detected and removed.

As discussed above, there are a number of differences between fiat money and cryptocurrency. Credit card users can cancel transactions done out of fraudulent activity. This is not possible with Bitcoin transactions as there is no way to cancel a transactions. Once your bitcoins are lost, there is no way to recover them. This is why you should take care of the private key in your wallet. In some cases, once you lose your fiat money, it is possible to get it back. If you had kept the money in your bank account, they may refund it depending on the bank's policy. However, if you had kept some cryptocurrency in your wallet and you lose it, no one will refund you.

Due to this property of cryptocurrencies, they offer the best option for use by hackers and other bad guys in society. They are sure that once they steal your money, there is no way you can recover it. Even viruses such as the WannaCry that encrypt the files of an organization demand that payment be made via Bitcoins in order to decrypt the files. This means the untraceable nature of cryptocurrencies is both an advantage and a disadvantage. Most Bitcoin thefts are the result of the mismanagement of the private key rather than failure of the underlying technology. If you mismanage the private key by making it known to someone else, they will be able to steal your Bitcoins and there is no way for you to recover them. There is no one or an organization you can blame or sue after losing your bitcoins, since the security of bitcoins relies solely on you as the owner. This is why you should always keep the private key secure.

Conclusion

The use and popularity of cryptocurrencies is on the rise. New cryptocurrencies are discovered every day. Bitcoin is known to be the first cryptocurrency in the entire world and it runs on the blockchain technology. Since the success of Bitcoin, several other cryptocurrencies have been developed and others are still under way. However, all of these cryptocurrencies rely on Bitcoin as a reference, and they are developed to fill in the gaps or solve its weaknesses. When making payments with cryptocurrencies, one is charged a lesser fee compared to making payments with fiat money.

Cryptocurrencies have also made it easy for banks, companies and individuals to make cross-border payments. Making cross-border payments with cryptocurrencies takes a short period of time compared to paying with fiat money. This is why most companies are now turning into cryptocurrencies as a means of payment. Note that cryptocurrencies do not exist in the form of notes or coins. They are just assets held digitally and secured by use of means of cryptography. A private key is used to authorize payments with cryptocurrencies. A public address is used to identify the account of a cryptocurrency user, meaning that other users must use it whenever they need to send money to the user.

In the real world, a government needs to print money whenever they need more in circulation. This is not the case with cryptocurrencies. To have more cryptocurrencies, a process known as mining must be done by users who have joined the cryptocurrency network known as *miners*. The miners are normally rewarded for their mining work which involves solving complex cryptographic puzzles. The process of mining is intensive in terms of electricity and

computation power.

www.ingramcontent.com/pod-product-compliance
Lightning Source LLC
Chambersburg PA
CBHW071207220526
45468CB00002B/523